Copyright © 2018 Anne Dupré

All rights reserved. No part of this book may be reproduced or transmitted in any form or by any means electronic or mechanical including photocopying, recording, or by any information storage and retrieval system without permission in writing from the publisher.

Aurora Books, an imprint of Eco-Justice Press, L.L.C.

Aurora Books
P.O. Box 5409 Eugene, OR 97405
www.ecojusticepress.com

The Brightest Star in the Sky
by Anne Dupré

Cover Design by David Diethelm | Eco-Justice Press
Cover Photo elements by Nathan Anderson, Don Kawahigashi, and Arnoldas Dogelis

Library of Congress Control Number: 2018936114
ISBN 978-1-945432-25-5

The Brightest Star in the Sky

For Dan, who journeys with me
from darkness to light

*The South-wind brings
Life, sunshine, and desire,*

. . . .

*But over the dead he has no power
And, looking over the hills, I mourn
The darling who shall not return.*

— *Emerson, Threnody*

Death does not discriminate and without warning Dan was gone. Why it should have happened when it happened I cannot say, but life as I had known it would never be the same.

The day began like so many nice days in early spring. A beam of sunlight slanted across the room, and a sparrow trilled its song in the blossoming kwanzan tree outside my bedroom window.

Rolled up on the floor at the foot of the bed was the Art Deco rug I had bought to surprise Dan. On our trip to the south of France when he was thirteen, he first become interested in Art Deco and was now decorating his new apartment in this period. I knew he was really going to like the rug.

Before leaving for my yoga class, I called Dan's cellphone to make sure he was coming to dinner that evening. There was no answer.

Several times during the day I called again. No answer. He must have forgotten his phone at home, I thought. I wasn't concerned,

In the late afternoon I started to prepare dinner. As I stirred the risotto and shiitake mushrooms, a favorite of Dan's, the sky darkened and then came the rain. The sound of the rain hitting the windowpane made me sad.

Curled up on her chair in the kitchen, our little pug dozed as she waited for the familiar click of Dan's key in the front door. When the aroma of mushrooms alerted her that Dan would be coming soon, she sat up and stared down the hallway. Just a whimper or two to let me know she was waiting, too.

At 5:20, the phone rang. Roger answered.

"Hello, Mr. Dupre, this is Don. Dan didn't come to work today and that's not like him, so I decided to stop by his apartment. I'm here now and his car is outside, but he's not answering the bell."

"Don, please call the landlady and have her let you into his apartment."

"OK. I'll call you back in a few minutes." Roger's face was tense. "Don is looking for Dan," he said.

I continued stirring the risotto.

The phone rang again.

After a long pause, Roger responded with a faint, "OK, Don." Then he put his arm around my shoulder and said, "Dan isn't well." Roger's eyes were deeply sad.

"What did Don say?" I was barely able to say the words.

"Dan's lying on the couch unconscious, but he's still breathing. Don's calling emergency at Flushing Hospital. He'll get back to us."

"Please God help Dan."

The phone rang again.

"The EMS team is taking Dan to Flushing Hospital," Don said.

"OK, Don. My wife and I will meet you there."

I left the risotto uncovered on the stove. As we hurried to the garage, I could hear Isabella's whimpers in the kitchen. We had forgotten to say goodbye. "We're busy, Izzie," I called out. "You be a good girl. We'll be back soon."

As we drove in silence, storm clouds darkened the sky, and the rain fell in torrents. A single light at the entrance to the hospital was blurred and dimmed by the heavy downpour.

"Emergency Room?" Hearing the urgency in Roger's voice, the nurse pointed quickly to the hallway on her right.

When we reached the ER, Roger ran in to Dan. For several minutes I remained frozen at the door. "Please God help Dan."

In a corner bed in a room filled with too many occupied beds, Dan lay unconscious surrounded by a team of doctors and nurses. All I could see were his toes pointing up to the ceiling. My mind flashed back to the last time I had seen Dan that way. Doctors were stitching up a gash over his eye that he had gotten from a pitch in a little league game. Then I was worried about a scar. Now I was hoping Dan would live.

The doctors worked on Dan through the night, and Roger stayed with him. On a metal folding chair in a room not much bigger than a closet, I waited alone. Sometimes I knelt on the tile floor. "Please God help Dan."

Toward dawn I remember we had forgotten to feed Isabella. Our diabetic pup needed to eat regularly.

When I went to call Roger, the doctors and nurses were still around Dan. I never really saw what they were doing. It was all too painful for me to watch.

"Do you think you should drive home to feed Izzie, Roger?"

"Why don't you drive with me, Anne? It won't take long."

"No, I can't leave Dan alone," I answered quickly. When Roger left, I returned to the little room as small as a confessional. "Please God help Dan."

At daybreak they moved Dan into intensive care. Roger and I waited together in a small visitors' room. Hours passed and we still didn't know whether Dan was going to live.

As the head doctor in intensive care hastened out the door, he said, "Don't worry. Your son will be up and about soon."

I sighed. Dan was going to be all right.

With confidence in her voice another doctor said as she quickly passed us in the hall, "We particularly take care of our young patients. We want them to go home walking."

Roger and I put our arms around each other. Dan was going to be all right.

What incredible asses those doctors were. The results of the brain scan showed that all Dan's cognitive functions were hopelessly gone.

"Why?" I asked the neurologist.

"Acute pulmonary failure," the doctor said.

At that moment I really didn't care what the doctor said. What could he say that would make Dan well again?

The next day we transferred Dan to NYU Langone Hospital.

April is the cruelest month.

— *T.S Eliot, The Wasteland*

It rained almost every day in April. The cherry blossom trees around our home were in full bloom, and I didn't care.

In the rainiest spring I can ever remember, Roger and I drove to Manhattan every day to be with Dan—hoping, praying. Family and dearest friends visited Dan, made dinners for Roger and me, and supported us in every way they could. But I needed the miracle, and the best neurologists in the city couldn't perform the miracle I was waiting for.

Dan never regained consciousness, and I never had the chance to say all the things I thought there'd be so much time to say. Dan died on May 8, 2009. He was only 28 years old.

Roger wrote: "On the twenty-fifth day, by his hospice bed in Calvary Hospital I talk to Dan. After some time—perhaps an hour—I lean forward. I say brokenly, 'I love you... No one ever had a better son... You're the best... But let go, Dan... Watch over your mother.'

Dan's eyes focus on mine intensely with a gaze of deep, deep compassion.

A single tear rolls down his cheek.

I leave and Anne and I take the long drive home. Soon after we arrive home, the doctor calls to say Dan had died."

Anne Dupré

The Tears ... streamed down, and I let them flow as freely as they could, making of them a pillow for my heart.

— Augustine, Confessions.

In the darkest moment of my life, I was not only sad but angry, even enraged.

Like King Lear's excruciating cry as he cradled the corpse of his daughter Cordelia in his arms, I wanted to hold Dan in my arms and shout: "No. No. No! It's wrong for Dan to die before me. He belongs to the future." I wept for all the living he would miss.

I remember reading about a head hunter tribe in a small village in the Philippines. Anthropologist Renato Rosaldo wrote that when a loved one died, the tribesman lay in the field waiting to behead the first person who came along. I understood this bereavement of rage too well.

No, I didn't behead anyone and in time, a long time, my anger subsided.

Anne Dupré

*Wandering between two worlds, one
dead The other powerless to be born,*
. . .
I wait forlorn.

— Matthew Arnold, *Stanzas from
the Grande Chartreuse*

In the fall I didn't return to teaching. Friends chatting, laughing, and exchanging ideas were too powerful an affirmation that life was going on without Dan. Returning to the classroom meant preparing young men like Dan to become productive members of society, a society Dan no longer inhabited.

I wanted to say "yes" to life. I knew Dan would want it that way. In turning to Eastern philosophies for comfort, I hoped to absorb their wisdom of compassion and mindfulness to the beauty around me. But our garden, bright all that spring and summer, didn't perform its magic. I needed more, so much more. As the air exploded with the sweet scent of Easter lilies and the cherry blossoms bloomed, I sat alone on the patio and the tears flowed.

Friends sent me books about grieving parents — moving books on grief and loss, but they didn't relieve my pain.

When I was finally able to contemplate, writing became my sanctuary. I wrote for several hours each day, usually before the sun came up. I wrote stories about the adventures of my little pug and her return in her dreams to a far-off time in ancient Tibet. They were tales of compassion and mindfulness.

I wrote stories about a boy with a wonderful imagination and a talent for writing stories. Stories that Dan should have written.

To banish the gloom of a rainy day in September eight years after Dan died, I curl up on the couch and read *The Child in the House*, Walter Pater's imaginary portrait of a young boy's awareness of the world around him. He writes:

"How significant seem the influence of the sensible things which are tossed and fall and lie about us in our childhood . . . How indelibly they affect us, giving form and feature to early experiences of feeling and thought that abide with us ever afterward . . . With the image of the place so clear . . he could watch the gradual expansion of his soul."

As I lie in bed, I hear Pater's whispers: "Revisit the beautiful memories you have of Dan and your heart will be full again."

In the morning I see Dan standing in front of the garage door waiting for Miss Isabella to arrive from the Canine Corners to her new home on Long Island. "She's a cute one, right Mom? Look at that monkey face and curly tail."

I have a picture of Dan holding the little pug like a football under his arm. With his care the little princess puppy would grow into a very fine princess lady, "Sit. Good Girl, Iz."

When Dan moved out, his weekly visits were always greeted with leaps and yelps and lots of lollipop licks from his little girl with a monkey face and a curly tail.

"Hold on Izzie. Be a good girl."

I never worried when Roger and I went away, Dan always took good care of Miss Isabella, and in her special puggily way she brought a great deal of love into Dan's life.

For a long time after Dan's death, Izzie curled up on her cushioned seat in the kitchen. Whining and whimpering softly, she stared longingly down the hall waiting for the familiar click of Dan's key in the front door.

As the memories begin to cast their spell, I know it is time to write Dan's story.

Anne Dupré

*Farewell to thee! but not farewell
To all my fondest thoughts of thee:
Within my heart they still shall dwell;
And they shall cheer and comfort me.*

— Anne Bronte, Farewell

The air has turned cold quickly this year. Surrounded by the mournful sound of an early winter wind, I sit down to write, and my journey out of hell begins.

We laughed. We cried. We loved. There were good times, wonderful times, and times that were difficult as well. Struggling to make sense of it all, I choose to remember the beautiful moments Dan and I shared.

As I sit on the patio in the mellow light of the sun's low slanting rays, only one hibiscus remains on the tree and the leaves are turning golden. The sound of the falling acorns from the oaks awakens the still melancholy of the end of summer. Beethoven's *Ninth* streams through the open patio door. Dan always loved Beethoven. "He's the man, Mom," he said.

How significant Beethoven or even the fragile fragrance of the purple-blue irises at the front door have become. In the early spring morning the beautiful blossoms stand tall reaching for the sky. "Hi, Mom, Happy Mother's Day."

These treasured memories tear down the cruel wall of mortality. They come as if in a dream, and as often happens in a dream, they rise a little above themselves.

Anne Dupré

Like the bright stars that illuminate a dark sky, their glow lights up my world. And the past becomes the now.

Long is the way and hard, that out of Hell leads up to light.

— *John Milton*

Even my earliest memory never grows dim. The window at Columbia Presbyterian Hospital looks out on a magnificent view of the Manhattan skyline. A moonbeam casts a fine line of light on the curves and angles of the metal bedstead, silver in the moonlight. The walls, painted a simple green, remind me of spring-time and hope, and the sweet, spicy scent of Roger's roses fills the room.

As I lie quietly matching my breath to the beeping of the machines in the hall, I recognize Daniel's cries. Hush, little baby. Please don't cry. Mommy's going to sing you a lullaby.

The nurse places Daniel in my arms. I sing, "I love you. Yes I do. You're the little boy that Mommy loves."

On the way home from the hospital, Roger turns on the radio to block out the screech of horns and sirens in Manhattan at noon. As we listen to the lovely andante movement of Mozart's *Piano Concerto no. 21*, Daniel curls his hand tightly around my finger and closes his eyes. "I'm going to take very good care of you, my darling."

After the storm on the day Dan died, a stunning band of soft pastels arch the horizon. My heart stands still as I follow the rainbow trail in the sky.

That evening Dan's dearest friend arrives at the wake holding a framed photo of the rainbow. With tears streaming down her face, she places the picture next to the tall white urn filled with purple-blue irises.

Today the rainbow has a prominent place on the credenza in our living room — a promise that Dan is here now and forever.

And so that's how it was in the beginning and in the end.

*There are no stars tonight
but those of memory.*

— Hart Crane.

On Friday evening I usually go to yoga class, but the biting wind and forecast of snow keeps me home tonight. As the bare branches of the kwanzan tree whip across the patio door, the wind-chime, which has become a citadel for my troubled heart, murmurs, "Now you can be with Dan."
    And so in the quiet of twilight, I follow the trail of memories in our home.
    Hidden in the corner of Dan's closet an old tennis racket stands without strings and without shame.
    "Why did you cut the strings, Dan?"
    "I just wanted to see what would happen," he said.
    That's so like Dan, I think. Unlike his dad Dan's interest never focused on tennis. He delighted in games of the imagination. His medieval knights still line up for battle on the shelf in his room. These childhood treasures filled his head with battles and heroes and foes.
    The jousting tournament at the Lyndhurst Castle in New Jersey brought to life an age that had only been words on a printed page, perhaps from the story of *St. George and the Dragon* he read so often.

While feasting on chicken eaten with our hands and sipping a mead-like concoction that tasted deliciously sweet, we watch the dazzling display of equestrian artistry.

Beside a glittering gilded Bay-tree the King and Queen in ermine capes and glimmering tiaras preside over the feast.

And then the drama begins. Adept at guiding their mounts through combat, the noble knights in full body armor, face visors, and iron helmets gallop into the arena on warhorses of great strength and stature. Draped in ornamental cloths, each Andalusian nobly wears his knight's heraldic emblem.

"Which one are you rooting for, Dad?"

At top speed, the knights charge in, thrusting their lances to unhorse their foes.

One knight, the Queen's favorite by the grimace on her face, is forced from his horse but continues sending fierce blows at his opponent.

"I'm glad I wasn't rooting for him," Dan says.

Taking advantage of the situation, the mounted adversary rains powerful blows on the head of the knight on foot.

"That's got to hurt, right Dad?"

The martial competition continues until one knight, his majesty's favorite, rides in glorious victory and bows before the King and Queen.

"That's the knight I was rooting for, Mom."

That summer Dan relives the pageant in our backyard. Racing across the wide spreading lawn and wielding his unsheathed plastic sword, he shouts fierce commands: "Stand, Sir, and receive your just reward for your lack of courage before the king."

Friend Cat peeks her striped head with big green eyes out of the pachysandra to watch the drama unfold.

On the top shelf of the closet an old shoe box contains some of Dan's boyhood mementoes: an old tennis ball, a pack of baseball cards, a few seashells, and several photographs of our trip to California. I cradle each photo in my hands.

Surrounded by a sweeping vista of the rugged Big Sur coastline, Dan stands on an isolated beach, his hair and jacket blowing in the wind. Behind him rocks sculptured by the forces of nature hold firm under the pounding of crashing waves.

Dan at Point Lobos State Reserve. As he kneels on a boulder and splashes one hand in a tidal pool to catch a turtle, a seagull swoops down to steal the frankfurter from his other hand.

Dan standing in front of a giant felled sequoia in the Mariposa Grove in Yosemite National Park. He looks so small.

Roger and Dan with the powerful presence of Half-Dome behind them illuminated by a fiery sunset of red and orange and gold.

Dan and I at Yosemite Falls. The raging waterfall cascades over the rocky cliffs, thundering down the mountain through the pine woods to the valley floor of wildflowers. We were close enough to feel the spray of water on our faces that day.

Dan in front of El Capitan. Rimmed by a ring of clouds, the giant granite monolith stands undisturbed by the skilled rock climbers challenged to reach its summit.

"Mom, why do you think the climbers risk their lives like that?"

Knowing now how precious life is, I certainly don't have an answer.

Although the memories may seem fragmentary in the way of half-remembered dreams, each photo works its magic, and even in winter roses bloom.

Anne Dupré

Write from recollection, and trust more to the imagination.

— *Samuel Taylor Coleridge*

On top of the piano a handsome cavalier stands tall to welcome the spirit of Christmas all year. Dan was only seven when we bought the wooden soldier at a performance of the *Nutcracker Ballet* which we attended each holiday season.

Holding the toy soldier in my hand, I suddenly imagine a stage with garlands of evergreens hanging from sparkling chandeliers and a Christmas tree glimmering in the glow of candlelight.

The image is clear. Dan looking so small in the big red velvet seat by my side.

As the tree reaches dizzying heights, Dan's eyes open wide. In a moonlit pine forest where ballerinas in silver-white tutus dance as delicately as silver-white snowflakes, I join Dan in the wonder that only a child knows and rise above ordinary retrospection. In this magical moment I am twelve years old and dancing on a small stage in a TV studio.

A beam of light slants across the stage and shines on a poor little match girl gazing longingly into a brightly lit window. It's the eve before Christmas and a family has gathered around a robust evergreen gleaming with candlelight. There are presents of warm woolen mittens and a doll in fine clothes and a bowl filled with candied apples and dried plums.

The glimmering tree fills the match girl with joy. Rising on pointe, the little waif dances as gracefully as the silver-white snowflakes swirling around her in the wind. Then the poor child curls up on a doorstep laden with snow and draws her legs close to keep out the harsh winter wind.

In a final effort to keep warm, her hands almost paralyzed with cold, the child lights all her remaining matchsticks. Each flickering flame holds a radiant image — presents wrapped in shiny gold paper with big red bows and children dancing merrily around a magnificent Christmas tree.

As the tree grows tall, the candles glisten like thousands of stars in the sky. Reaching for the glow of each quivering light, the little match girl dances as if held up by angel's wings.

My childhood dream-vision and my memories of Dan intertwine in unexpected ways and shine a special light into the darkness.

Music gives a soul to the universe.

— Plato

It had been raining all afternoon and showed no promise of stopping very soon.

"Let's go and pick up Grandma," my father says.

When we arrive, Grandma is standing under the marquee of the Brooklyn Academy of Music. On the carved stone façade behind her, the poster of a flaming red candle shining on a beautiful white camellia brightens the gray day.

"*La Traviata* is Grandma's favorite opera," Dad says.

Every Sunday afternoon in springtime my grandmother always attended her beloved operas.

I loved the opera as well. In season Roger and I went often to the Met, and on Saturday afternoons I listened to the opera on the radio. The triumphant march from *Aida* always stirred fond memories.

"My mother named me Aida after her favorite opera," Mom said.

Even in the dark, music casts its spell. When I was a child and the light from the street lamp outside my bedroom window shone on my magic skin doll and brown teddy bear, forming long, dark shadows on the wall, I was a little afraid. But I never felt alone when I played *Sleeping Beauty* on the pink record player Aunt Rose gave me. I wanted Dan to experience the magic music creates.

Each night after Roger read *Sand Cakes*, Dan's favorite bedtime story, I played Mozart's *Concerto no. 21* until he fell asleep. The lovely andante movement always worked its magic.

Then on a summer day, the kind of day when the paved roads give up a haze, Dan's serious musical journey began.

In a sun-filled room overlooking Hempstead Harbor, a pale lilac-grey Siamese peeks her head from behind the couch, and a chestnut tabby stares suspiciously from the top of a shiny black piano.

Six years old is a perfect age to start Suzuki," Miss Wendy says and shakes Dan's hand.

"Do you like cats, Dan?"

"What are the cats' names?"

"Sasha and Tikki"

"I have a cat named Friend Cat."

Sasha curls up on Miss Wendy's lap as she plays *Twinkle, Twinkle Little Star*. Dan follows her fingers as they move across the black and white keys glistening in the sunlight and repeats Mozart's little gem. I marvel at the ease and quickness in which he learns.

"I like Miss Wendy and I want to take piano lessons, Mom," Dan says on the drive home. "Aren't the cats nice?"

Is it Wendy or Sasha and Tikki or even the shiny black Kawai glistening in the sunlight that wins Dan's heart? I wonder.

On a treeless street in Brooklyn when I was already twelve, I pull open the heavy glass and wrought iron door to Miss Trombell's apartment building.

"Come in Anne dear," a frail woman in a white tailored blouse greets me at her door.

In the protracted light of the lengthening day before the warm weather began, I sit down at an old upright piano in the corner of a dimly lit and darkly paneled room. No black and white keys glistening in the sunlight or Mozart's gem to cast its spell or even Sasha and Tikki to welcome me that day.

Miss Trombell guides me through the scales: C D E F G A B C. The monotonous sound of my untrained fingers as they move slowly up and down the ivory keys, dull with age, compete with the laughter of friends engaged in a vigorous game of stick ball outside the open window.

By summer I learn to follow the commanding tick and tock of the metronome, and my repertoire includes *Take Me Out to the Ballgame*, one of Dad's favorites. Dad settles in the old green velvet chair next to the spinet and sings along. His robust voice, sometimes off key, drowns out my playing, but I don't care. This moment is my special time with Dad.

When Dan played, I often sat on a folding chair next to the old walnut spinet. There was no singing along at all.

"That's lovely, Dan. Please play it again."

In the Suzuki tradition Miss Wendy introduced Dan to Beethoven and Bach and Mozart from the very beginning.

On a summer's day when even the birds are silent, a sun-filled auditorium buzzes with the chatter of family and friends. Wendy puts her arm around Dan's shoulder and whispers, "You're going to do a great job today, Dan." He gives her one of those big smiles I love so much.

"Now Daniel, our youngest performer, will play Beethoven's *Sonata, no. 29.*"

In a blue blazer and red tie, one of the few occasions when he isn't wearing jeans, Dan walks across the floor, bows, and sits down on the stool that Wendy had to adjust for his height.

Raising his hands above the keyboard, he pauses and glances over to Roger and me. Before his feet can reach the pedals or his hands span an octave, his fingers race across the keyboard. Even at eight years old performing comes so naturally.

Dan loved playing the piano. In his early teen years, when school and friends and street hockey filled his day, he always found time to play a piece or two. Sometimes when the house is quiet, I hear the strains of Joplin's *The Entertainer*.

When you passed an open window on Park Place at dusk on a summer's day many years ago, you might have heard Beethoven's *Fur Elise*, Mom's favorite, or Hoagy Carmichael's *Stardust*, Dad's sing-along preference.

I smile when I think of Mom's plan to keep me practicing each day. "Anne," she said as she rose from the dinner table, "I'll do the dishes while you play the piano."

Accompanied by the steady beat of the metronome, the sound of the water running was an unstated command that I continue playing.

One evening anxious for the practice to end, I go into the kitchen to plead my case. "Mom, I've been practicing for a half hour."

The faucet is still running, but Mom's nowhere in sight.

Although music remained an important part of my life, I didn't have the talent or interest in piano that Dan had. My dream was to become a prima ballerina someday.

Waiting in the wings, I hear the murmur of the audience and the rustling of settling in. In the breathless quiet when the house lights dim, my heart races even as I will it to be still.

The music from the pit swells and the curtain rises. With my arms poised in first position, I rise on pointe and pas de bourrée into the spotlight in my yellow organza ballerina dress Mom made for me.

As I sweep across the stage "To the beat, beat, beat of the tom, tom" and the "drip, drip, drip of the raindrops" of my first ballet solo *Night and Day*," my fear disappears and

I step into the enchantment of dance.

"What did you think, Mom?"

"I told you the dress would be great. You looked lovely tonight, Anne."

Those weren't exactly the words I wanted to hear, but Mom never encouraged my dancing dream.

As darkness falls fast, once more my imagination takes flight and Dan is near. There are no stars tonight, only the moon shining through the living room window. Bathed in the moonlight, the bust of Beethoven we gave Dan on his sixteenth birthday stands guard.

Then the sound of music.

Dan's firm muscular body sways from side to side as he strokes the pianissimos and drives out the fortes of the beautiful *Moonlight Sonata*. In the musical theater in his mind, Beethoven is the man.

Since Dan's death, music enables me to experience feelings and thoughts I never had before. At a recent concert my heart has wings.

As the concert hall darkens, I hope the darkness will hide my tears. Every note in Beethoven's *Ninth Symphony* rings out with emotional hope. At the glorious "Ode to Joy," the tears and darkness disappear. "He's the man, Mom."

Beethoven's words have great significance now: "Only Art," he says," makes us suspect the existence of life on a higher level."

Then when the somber bass note of Mozart's *Piano Sonata K22* asks a profound question, there are no answers. The musical voice's only response is another question. Always the questions remain unresolved.

Composed after the death of his infant son, the sonata reflects a soul searching for answers.

I understand. There are so many questions I want answered.

Anne Dupré

The program note includes Mozart's words: "As death, when we come to consider it closely, is the true goal of our existence, I have formed during the last few years such close relationships with this best and truest friend of mankind that death's image is not only no longer terrifying to me, but indeed very soothing and consoling."
I try to make sense of it all. Perhaps in time I will.

Life starts all over again when it gets crisp in the fall.

— F. Scott Fitzgerald

Today I stop to admire the impatience, still robust and in full bloom all around the house in October. I'm beginning to notice the beauty in my garden again.

As the summer edges toward fall and the last hibiscus withers and drops to the ground, I love watching the leaves change into astonishing colors of gold and russet and red. The resplendent foliage reminds me that Mozart's *Requiem* is back in town.

Each year Roger and I go to the Philharmonic to honor Dan. The devastating beauty of the *Requiem* brings me to a place where the world and eternity meet. In a deeply moving way music connects me to Dan now.

Anne Dupré

The artist is the hand that . . . causes vibrations in the soul.

— Kandinsky

Two fine prints in Mucha's distinctive Art Nouveau style hung in Mom and Dad's bedroom the entire time I was growing up. I really didn't pay very much attention to them.

When Mom and Dad passed, the pictures came to our home. Dan always loved the lovely dreamy-eyed ladies surrounded by an elaborate array of chrysanthemums and lilies and pale-yellow daisies.

For all too brief a time the ladies in robes as blue as the water of the Mediterranean hung in Dan's apartment above his couch and next to his photo of the Chrysler skyscraper, an iconic Art Deco design.

Now the lovely ladies have come back home to reconnect me to Dan and to Mom and to Dad.

Although the undelivered present of the Art Deco rug has been returned to the store, the memory of Dan's interest in art remains.

On a clear, moonlit evening, Dan and I stroll the Promenade des Anglais. The crescent curve of the beach under the starry night stretches out before us.

"The view looks like a painting," Dan says.

Dan is right, the scene looks very much like Van Gogh's *Starry Night over the Rhone*, I think.

Today when I look at Van Gogh's *Starry Night Over the*

Anne Dupré

Rhone above my desk, I see Dan strolling beside me along the Promenade des Anglais with the crescent curve of the beach stretching out before us.

In the summer of 2007 we travel to Florence, Italy. Crowds gather to look at Ghiberti's bronze doors on the main entrance to the Baptistry in front of the Cathedral of Santa Maria del Flore.

"Michelangelo named the glorious doors the Gates of Paradise, Dan. These narrative reliefs of the Old Testament are a compelling testament to Ghiberti's genius."

As the soft, golden hues of a summer twilight create the illusion of deep space, Dan catches the striking beauty of the magnificent doors on his cellphone.

At home on the wall in the hall, Dan's photo of *The Death of St Francis* captures the profound and moving beauty of Giotto's masterpiece. Words alone cannot do justice to this unparalleled fresco in the Basilica of Santa Croce — St. Francis's disciples gathered for his funeral. One mourner kisses the stigmata and another watches the saint's soul being carried heavenward by angels.

Dan's stately elm, limbs black and rimmed with snow, hung in the principal's office through the school year and now hangs above our fireplace. In a story I wrote about a boy very much like Dan I included some of his paintings. Dan always loved to paint and draw.

"Dan had a stellar eye and a great sense of color," his colleague at the photography studio told me at his wake.

I am acquainted with no immaterial sensuality so delightful as good acting.

— *Lord Byron*

"Mom, I think I want to be an actor."
Performing was in Dan's genes. My dad loved to sing and dance. Even when I barely reached his waist, I was Dad's favorite dancing partner at family weddings. As I struggled to keep my patent leather Mary Janes from slipping off Dad's shoes, he twirled me around the dance floor until the band went home.
Although Dad didn't play a fiddle, he certainly knew how to win his little girl's heart. Sometimes at sunset or even at sunrise on summer days, we walked hand in hand around the backyard admiring Mom's pink peonies and cherry-red geraniums. Then for no reason at all, Dad burst into song: "Is this the little girl I carried? When did she get to be a beauty? When did she grow to be so tall?"
No, Dad never did make it to Broadway, but Roger had his brief moment in the limelight.
In the summer rain falls suddenly almost every afternoon in Orlando, Florida. Having forgotten our rain slickers at the hotel, we step into Universal Studios for shelter. The crew is casting for *The Man in the Gray Pinstripe Suit*, and they choose Roger for the leading role.
Reluctant at first to be in the spotlight, Detective Dupré

in a fedora and trench coat speaks his lines "trippingly on the tongue," bows, and hurries off stage.

"Congratulations, Dad." Roger is Dan's role model today.

"Mom, I think I want to become an actor," he announces on our plane ride back to Long Island.

At home his loyal companion shares the limelight with him. Turning Friend Cat upside down and holding her tail to his mouth like a microphone, he walks around the house singing, "You're just a silly little girl with a long, thin tail. You're a rock and roll cat." – The tabby never objects to her moments of fame.

But Dan's debut at the Christmas pageant in pre-school does not go well at all.

"Mom, are you coming to school today?"

"Of course, Dan. I'll be there."

The scent of pine fills the air and bells and holly and wreaths are everywhere. In the wings I see Dan and his classmates in their bobbled Santa hats waiting patiently to close the pageant.

For weeks the children had been decorating their cardboard train with all shapes and sizes of carrot-nosed snowmen in stovepipe hats. When the train roars onto the stage – Choo, Choo. Choo, Choo. –tears stream down Dan's face.

Mrs. Monroe picks him up and carries him over to me. "When he's ready, he'll let go," she says.

She's right. "The readiness is all." From kindergarten on performing comes so naturally to Dan.

But his performance as first cellist in the Christmas concert in his freshman year in junior high does not go the way I hoped. Although he plays well and there are no tears, he's pretty darned annoyed with me.

"Mom, I'm never wearing this suit again."

The suit didn't fit well, I have to admit. And knowing

Dan, I should have expected this reaction.

But his performance in *The Odd Couple* in high school is a smashing success.

"Mom, are you coming to see the play tonight?"

"Of course, Dan. Dad and I will be there.'".

Oscar Madison, the unkempt, carefree sportswriter is pretty out of character for Dan, but he plays his part well.

"Life goes on, even for those of us who are divorced, broke, and sloppy." Dan spoke his lines as Hamlet would have him, suiting "the action to the word, the word to the action . . . and he did "not saw the air too much with his hand."

As the curtain closes, Roger and I join the cacophony of applause and whistles and cheers.

"Bravo, Dan."

"See you later," and he dashes off to the cast party.

Dan loved it all. Performing was in his genes.

Anne Dupré

An emotion has found its thought and the thought has found words.

— *Robert Frost*

When the light in Dan's room shone late into the night, I knew he was writing. Even as I met with Dan's third grade teacher to discuss his daydreaming in class, I would pass his award-winning story on the bulletin board in the hall outside his classroom.

This morning as I gather some of Dan's clothes and videos to give to the Glen Boy's Club, I come across a draft of an article he was writing for the *Viking Voice*, his high school newspaper. Throwing his favorite brown leather bomber jacket with the scent of Boss cologne still lingering over my shoulder, I hold the fraying article carefully.

1996-1997 Islander by Dan Dupré

Although it may take a miracle for the New York Islanders hockey team to make it to the playoffs this year, they do have one great asset: youth. With an average team age of only twenty-five years old, they are full of great potential.

One of these new talented players is Brian Berard, who was acquired by the Islanders from the Ottawa Senators late last season after being selected number one overall in

Anne Dupré

the 1994-1995 National Hockey League (NFL) draft. Many hockey scouts compare this nineteen-year old defensemen's fluid puck control and offensive prowess to the Rangers' Brian Leetch and the Islanders' legend and Hall of Famer Denis Potvin.

The Islanders' potential, however, does not end with Berard. Zisgmund Palffy, the premier player of this youthful organization led the Islanders last year with 43 goals and 87 points. Defenseman Kenny Jonsson's heads up passing is helping in odd man rushes, and right-Winger Todd Bertuzzi strength on his feet gives the Islanders muscle around the goal.

The Islanders may not make it to the playoffs this season, but with sufficient progress and development, they could once again become a Stanley Cup contender in the next couple of years.

* * *

"Dad, can you believe the Islanders finished 12 points short of the playoffs this season?" he asked that year.

This morning Roger told me Dan would have been happy to hear that in 2016 the Islanders defeated the Florida Panthers to finally win their first playoff series since 1993.

In the drawer next to the sport's article I found a couple of pages of Dan's assignment to create a new ending for *The Catcher in the Rye*. Dan was in ninth grade, and Salinger really captured his imagination that year.

On the top page, dated January 15, 1995, his teacher wrote, "Tone and character are so authentic that it seems as if Salinger is writing again. The humor is terrific. This is outstanding writing."

Holden's Born Again

After I convinced Phoebe to stay with the family instead of leaving with me, I took her to the movies. You know, because I was sorry and all. As we walked along 23rd Street, the only theaters open were those damned porno XX cinemas. So all we really ended up doing was taking a walk. A walk for Christ's sake. In the middle of the freakin' night.

Anyway, it was 3 in the morning, but the city was lit up with all the lights from those shops that think they can make another stupid buck by keeping on a freakin' neon sign. Three in the morning, can you believe it. Mr. Antolini kept me at his house for about a million hours. You know, because he was trying to explain why he touched me. I thought I knew him. I got out of his house about two in the morning. Anyway, I took a walk with Phoebe down to Pathmark because it was open 24 hours and all. I don't see how anyone could stand that damn graveyard shift. It kills me, it really does. Anyway, we walked in and I bought Phoebe one of those Snickers bars. She's crazy about those, she really is. I was gonna get some beer but I figured I had enough. Just coming from Mr. Antolini's and all. That damn pervert. When we got out of Pathmark, we walked around for a while.

"Holden," Phoebe asked. "Why do ya have to do it?"

"Do what?" I asked.

"Why do you have to leave, of course," she said.

Phoebe gets pretty obnoxious sometimes, but I love her anyway. I really do.

"Come on, Phoebe," I retorted. "We've gone through this before. I have no direction, nowhere to go in life. At least you have friends. Who the hell do I have, Ackley? I'm a damn loser. I need to find myself."

"Well, if you have to go," Phoebe began, "then why can't you take me. I just turned ten you know. I can take care of myself. I won't be any trouble, I promise. I cross my heart and h...."

"Oh, just shut up with that crap. That stuff is the last thing I need to hear right now. You're not going, and I don't want to hear any more about it. I just want some place where I can get away from life for a while. You just wouldn't fit in."

"That's it." Phoebe said. "I can't take this anymore. I'm going."

Phoebe threw down her half-eaten Snickers bar and ran to the corner. Before I could stop her, she had hailed a taxi and was on her way back to the house. She left me standing there, didn't even say goodbye.

* * *

"It's not fair." Dan died at the beginning of a creative life that held so much promise.

"I got in, Mom." Dan leaps into the kitchen waving a large yellow envelope in the air. I shake his hand and give him a big hug.

NYU's Tisch School of Dramatic Writing was an excellent college for Dan's talent to expand.

"The class gave my film *The Volvo of Discontent* a standing ovation, Mom."

"Bravo, Dan!"

Dan's career in writing and filmmaking was just beginning.

As I try to regain my balance, I tell myself Dan had found his passion. He was doing what he loved. "This is my year to shine," he told a friend.

*Failing to fetch me at first, keep encouraged.
Missing me one place, search another.
I stop somewhere, waiting for you.*

— *Walt Whitman, Song of Myself*

Wherever my thoughts go, Dan is there.

In Busch Gardens, Virginia a majestic bald eagle with a massive hooked beak soars through the air like a burst of lightening and curls his powerful talons on his keeper's arm. His piercing eyes are staring at Dan.

At the Cold Spring Harbor Fish Hatchery a steelhead trout with a horizontal pinkish stripe swims towards Dan.

"Rainbow trout have sharp teeth," Roger warns. But Dan dangles his hand into the pond anyway.

"Ouch," he cries out.

That's so like Dan, I think.

In the lush vegetation of the Congo Gorilla Forest in the Bronx Zoo, a group of apes knuckle-walk clumsily through the dense evergreens and hemlock trees. Distinguished by the glistening steak of silver hair down his back, the dominant silverback sits in command, posing long enough for Dan to take his picture.

A rainbow of brilliant colors sweeps across the glass roof in the Serengeti Plains at Busch Gardens, Tampa Bay. There are white-eyed lovebirds and brightly colored hornbills and parrots with red and yellow tails. Dan holds a cup of fruit nectar in his outstretched arm and a black knobbed

Anne Dupré

hornbill with a yellow-orange beak settles right down on his head.
And so in winter roses still bloom.

*What cannot be seen with the eye.
But that whereby the eye can see:
Know that alone . . . be the eternal spirit.*

— *The Upanishads*

"This morning I saw the country from my window a long time before sunrise, with nothing but the morning star, which looked very big," Van Gogh wrote to his brother Theo.

Standing before the picture of Van Gogh's *Starry Night*, I know my journey with Dan is just beginning. *Starry Night* points the way.

Rooted in Van Gogh's imagination as a homage to nature, the painting transcends traditional religion.

Anne Dupré

Presiding over the village church in the distance, a large flame-like cypress unites the churning sky with the quiet hamlet below.

As I follow the dark, curving branches of the flame-shaped tree, I journey through the cycle of life and death. Traveling with the stars swirling over rolling hills and the golden moon pulsating in an orb of yellow light, I see Dan in a place where the moon and the stars are radiant.

Behold, I have dreamed a dream more;
and, behold the sun and the moon and
the eleven stars made obeisance to me.

— *Genesis 37:9*

"You know who you are, you are the shining star."

—Rumi

Today I celebrate Dan and his consanguinity with the natural beauty surrounding us.
    At sunrise a silver-studded butterfly quivers around a purple-blue iris. I watch its fluttering wings dance in the golden light.
    This year the hibiscus has spectacular blooms. I cradle one of the fragile blossoms in my hand and gather a few pale-yellow daisies.
    "Mom, here are some daisies I picked for you."
    At twilight a moonbeam slants across the room, and the sparrow trills its song in the blossoming kwanzan tree. I stop to look at the blossoms and see the sparrow soaring up to the tall oak reaching for the clouds.
    The earth's brightest star illuminates the sky tonight, and I dream.

Anne Dupré

Epilogue

*To hope till Hope creates
From its own wreck the thing it
contemplates; Neither to change, nor
falter, nor repent; This, like the glory,
Titan, is to be Good, great and joyous,
beautiful and free; This is alone Life, Joy,
Empire, and Victory!*

— Shelley, Prometheus Unbound

www.ingramcontent.com/pod-product-compliance
Lightning Source LLC
Chambersburg PA
CBHW071546080526
44588CB00011B/1809